I0420126

INFJ Personality:

Shape Your Ultimate Dream Life by Understanding Your Uniqueness

Copyright © 2015 Jacky Ye

Contents

Introduction

I would like to thank you and congratulate you for downloading the book, *"INFJ Personality: Shape Your Ultimate Dream Life by Understanding Your Uniqueness."*

This book contains proven steps and strategies on how to understand the INFJ personality type and what steps you should take to maximize your potential and to live in the world as a successful INFJ.

Do you often feel as though you're all alone? Do you believe that you are often misunderstood? INFJs are known to be the rarest of the 16 personality types. They are also known to possess the greatest potential to create a huge change in the world. But before you can do that, you need to understand the strengths of your personality as well as its weaknesses.

If you've just found out that you belong in this rare type, your head is probably swarming with questions like: *What's the big deal?* And more importantly: *What do I do?* This book aims to answer all these questions and more. You'll be able to explore the different facets of the INFJ through the roles that they play in the society—as a friend, as a lover, as a parent, as a boss, as a worker, as a colleague, and as a person in general. More than that, you'll learn how an INFJ can improve himself/herself in these various areas. Furthermore, this book also contains additional tips to non-INFJ types who want to understand, make friends with, and/or fall in love with someone with an INFJ personality.

Are you having a hard time finding your place in the world? Is it difficult for you to find a satisfying job? That's because INFJs view success differently from other personality types. In the last chapters, you'll learn which careers are perfect for the INFJ personality so that you can find *and* maintain a meaningful job that fulfills you as a person.

Chapter 1: Understanding the INFJ

"Your visions will become clear only when you can look into your own heart. Who looks outside, dreams; who looks inside, awakes." - Carl Jung, a famous INFJ

What is the INFJ?

The INFJ is an abbreviation used to indicate one of the sixteen personality types in the Myer-Briggs Type Indicator, otherwise known as MBTI. The MBTI is a psychometric questionnaire engineered by Katharine Cook Briggs and Isabel Briggs Myers to assess people's psychological preferences. It reflects how an individual perceives his environment and how he formulates his decisions. Briggs and Myers designed the questionnaire based on Carl Jung's theory of four principal psychological functions. According to Jung, a person experiences the world through thinking, intuition, sensation, and feeling. Additionally, he theorized that at most times, one of these functions tend to be more dominant than the others. INFJ stands for Introversion, iNtuition, Feeling and Judging.

Dissecting the INFJ

- **Introverted Intuition**

Compared to other personality types, and with the exception of the INTJs, INFJs possess a clearer perception of their internal, instinctive processes. A person with the INFJ personality is able to easily comprehend the concealed psychological stimuli behind the more obvious subtleties of behavior. INFJs have an amazing skill for deduction. For this reason, plenty of people with this personality type turn out to be prophets or psychics. Whereas Introverted Sensing tends to be routine in nature, Introverted Intuition is characterized by more spontaneous, insightful actions.

- **Extraverted Feeling**

In INFJs, this secondary function depicts a spectrum of emotions and ideas *of*, *for*, as well as *about* others. The thing about INFJs is that they possess the desire to express their prolific ideas and moral deductions concerning other people's behavior. However, they are also deeply aware of the consequences of unrestricted openness. As a result, INFJs share their feelings privately to carefully chosen confidantes. This is because INJFJs have a deep awareness of human beings' capacity for deceit. This extraverted secondary function coupled with the primary function (Introverted Intuition) is the reason why INFJs have the makings of great counselors.

- **Introverted Thinking**

Thinking, which is the INFJs tertiary function tend to be less efficient than the two functions mentioned above. For this reason, a INFJs thinking have a tendency to revolve around the subject, making him seem detached. When an INFJ is concentrating his energy on his thoughts, an observer might wrongly perceive him as being indifferent.

- **Extraverted Sensing**

One of the greatest features of INFJs is that they possess clarity of both internal and external vision. However, compared to the other functions, sensing tends to be the least dominant and the most vulnerable. As a result, when a person with the INFJ personality becomes too immersed in his intuitive observations, he may become unmindful of external realities. When in a vulnerable state, an INFJ may easily be tempted to indulge in different means of immediate gratification. Furthermore, INFJs awareness of extraverted sensing may lead them to emulate the SP personality, that is, they yearn for freedom and despise being tied down. They live life on a day-to-day basis with a *desire* for impulsiveness and minimal thought of the future.

Are you really an INFJ?

- *Do you find yourself being aware of certain information without knowing how you came to know it?*

- *Do you often trust your intuition when making decisions? Does it often lead to favorable outcomes?*

- *Do you frequently feel that you're profoundly misunderstood?*

- *Do you prefer hobbies that enable you to express yourself?*

- *Do you tend to ponder about the world?*

- *Do you enjoy structure and do you tend to plan ahead?*

- *Are you sensitive? When you're emotionally stressed, can you feel it in your body as well?*

- *Do you find it easy to empathize with other people?*

- *Do people often turn to you for advice?*

- *Do you prefer interacting with people on a one-on-one basis than on a mass scale?*

- *Do you prefer keeping only a handful of friends that you love fiercely?*

- *Do you think that deep, genuine initial connection a prerequisite for friendship?*

- *Do you find it difficult to find someone who's very much like you?*

- *Do you prioritize relationships? And do you feel like most of your relationships are one-sided?*

If your answer to these questions is yes, then it's likely that you are an INFJ.

What does the INFJ look like?

INFJs have a tendency to dress up in an orthodox fashion with the goal of being socially appropriate. Meanwhile, their J (Judging) personality pushes them to become extra careful about their physical appearance.

What makes the INFJ special?

The INFJ personality is known to make up less than 1% of the population and thus, making it the rarest of personality types. Famous INFJS include Gandhi, Chaucer, Martin Luther King Jr., Emily Bronte, Thomas Jefferson, Mother Teresa of Calcutta, and Carl Jung himself.

INFJs are idealists and moralists (NF). But more than that, they also possess a judging characteristic (J) which yearn for completion and conclusion. This trait prevents people with this personality trait for being idle dreamers. So instead, INFJs have the capacity to become doers who have the power to influence the world and leave behind their legacy.

The INFJs character is, to put it plainly, very complex. People who possess the INFJ personality possess talents, which are uncommon in terms of breadth and depth. INFJs are special in such a way that their personalities are a concoction of conflicting characteristics that somehow seem to work. For instance, INFJs tend to be soft-spoken individuals. Yet, at the same time, they also possess strong opinions and ideals, which they are not afraid to fight for to the end. They possess strength of will and the potential to become truly influential. But instead of utilizing this to benefit themselves, they choose compassion and act with conviction. INFJs act with creativity not to advance themselves but in order to achieve balance. Karma, equality—these are all ideas that INFJs find appealing because of their strong humanitarian outlook.

What are the INFJs strengths?

- INFJs are creative. And they apply this creativity to fixing human challenges instead of technical ones. Simply put, they are natural born problem-solvers.

- INFJs are perceptive. They are easily able to see through people and identify their motives. Furthermore, they can determine with little difficulty the connection between the circumstances and the persons involved. As a result, they are less likely to become victims of dishonesty. They prefer open discussion to sales talk.

- INFJs are motivational and persuasive. This is because of their innate ability to communicate through human terms as opposed to technical terms. INFJ writers possess a fluid style that engages the idealist side of the reader. Despite being introverts, INFJs may turn out to be great public speakers especially if they are passionate about the subject.

- INFJs are decisive. Creativity, intuition, inspiration, determination, and the ability to plan are all characteristics that make the INFJ ideal candidates for shaping the world. They not only see things as they should be but they also act based on that awareness.

- INFJs are passionate. People with this type of personality may often surprise even their closest intimates once they pursue something that they truly believe in.

- INFJs are unselfish and humane. One of the best things about persons with this type of personality is that when they perform good deeds, they do it not for egotistical reasons but because they truly believe that the act can improve the world.

What are the INFJ's weaknesses?

- INFJs are sensitive. The surest and quickest way to piss off an INFJ is to challenge his motives. People with this personality type hate conflict and have a tendency to take criticisms personally.

- INFJs are exceedingly private individuals. Even their friends may find it difficult to persuade them to open up.

- INFJs tend to be perfectionists. This often leads to frustration and disappointments. They may even forsake healthy relationships (whether personal or business in nature) because they believe that there's something out there that better fits into their ideals.

What to Do If You're an INFJ

INFJs are prone to burnout. The thing about INFJs is that they unconsciously *absorb* other people's emotions. This goes one step beyond human empathy and ultimately, it's what makes them wonderful counselors. But this can also easily lead to emotional overload. Furthermore, individuals of this personality type have poor tolerance for routine. If you're an INFJ, you need to be able to manage your expectations when it comes to relationships. Furthermore, you need to be able to balance your ideals with the realities of daily life.

Another typical feature of INFJs is that they feel naturally drawn towards certain responsibilities. If you're an INFJ, you may feel that the world is needlessly governed by inequity. And true enough, your personality type has what it takes to truly right the wrongs in this world, whether they're major or minor. However, you also need to remember that your passion can easily lead to exhaustion and thus, you mustn't neglect to take care of yourself. Otherwise, in the face of struggle or when surrounded by criticism, your sensitivity may lead you to fight back in an illogical manner. Or you might end up doing everything in your power to avoid the attack which to you seems very personal even when it's not.

"In a gentle way, you can shake the world." - Gandhi, a famous INFJ

Chapter 2: INFJ and Friendship

"A man can be himself only so long as he is alone; and if he does not love solitude, he will not love freedom; for it is only when he is alone that he is really free." - Arthur Schopenhauer, a famous INFJ

What do INFJs look for in a friend?

There are two things that INFJs look for when it comes to friendships and any type of relationships and those are:

- Sincerity
- Authenticity

If you're an INFJ then it's unlikely for you to form friendships by circumstance (ex. in the workplace/ neighborhood). That's because the fact that they relate with someone on a daily basis is not enough common ground for an INFJ to consider building a friendship. INFJs look for an instant, almost miraculous connection upon contact. To them, potential friends are individuals who share the same interests and ideologies as theirs. They want someone with whom they can explore ideas and themes that they find important. Finding friendship for INFJs is really more about looking for a soul mate.

Basically, INFJs are looking for is someone that they can *grow* with. In fact, an INFJ can thrive on having just one person as a companion and he will not feel like he's missing out on other relationships at all. That said, compared to other introverts who can be perfectly fine on their own, INFJs actually do better with other people around. In the absence of a close relationship, an INFJ may feel a sense of emptiness. Prolonged solitude may even lead to depression. In summary, the INFJ's social needs can only be satisfied through emotional and intimate connections with a few very well-chosen friends and family members.

What's it like to be friends with an INFJ?

With regards to communication, INFJs possess a skill for warmth, empathy, and subtlety that it's easy for them to connect with others. When you're speaking with an INFJ, you feel like he is really listening to you and that he really cares. He refrains from judging you too easily. And yet, there are times when he may seem aloof in his communication. At these times, it is important to understand that he is simply sorting out his thoughts and feelings.

Strangely enough, friends of INFJs regard them as "quiet extroverts". One reason why an inherently introvert INFJ can be mistaken for an extrovert is because he tends to care a lot about his relations with individuals. In fact, he cares a lot about the state of humanity in general. This genuine interest in people, which is a result by their Feeling function, causes them to be mistaken for socializers.

Friends of people with this type of personality are likely to observe their friend withdrawing from them from time to time. This is because INFJs are inherent givers and this makes them prone to emotional overload. Therefore, they require some time to be alone in order to recharge their energies. To outsiders, this singular feature can be quite confusing. Some people might take this the wrong way and this is one of the reasons why INFJs are so often misunderstood.

If you're a friend of someone with an INFJ personality, it is important to understand that this detachment is momentary and has nothing to do with you personally. In fact, your friend is detaching himself not just from you but from the rest of the world. The thing is, individuals who possess this personality type have a high regard and a deep concern for other people's feelings and in turn, they also expect others to do the same for them. This might mean occasionally providing them with some breathing space.

Lastly, the best thing about being a friend of the INFJ is that when they do form friendships, it's for the long haul. They are nurturing and encouraging and can provide you with life-enriching experiences. Since they're good conversationalists, you can talk with them about just about anything. People of this personality type are extremely loyal. They are sincere about caring for you and may even take it as their responsibility to help you find solutions to your problems. An INFJ will do just about anything to keep you in his life, even adapt himself in order to ensure your happiness.

How to Be Friends with an INFJ

- Make the first move. Keep in mind that INFJs are unlikely to initiate the conversation.

- Make sure that your motive is sincere. INFJs can easily pick up incongruence in verbal and non-verbal cues. Once they suspect you of being insincere, they'll simply dismiss you. Even when you see each other on a regular basis, they'll maintain their distance by keeping conversations civil but without truly revealing anything.

- Be patient. So you've made the first move. You've been honest so far. So why is your INFJ friend still not opening up? The answer is it takes a great deal of time and patience to peel back the layers of the INFJ. Basically, an INFJ will look at you and determine whether or not you fit into his life. If he sees a possibility, he might bend his rules to let you in.

- Avoid interrupting INFJs while they're trying to express themselves. Otherwise, they'll feel like you're disinterested and this will prevent them from sharing with you in the future.

- Lastly, never betray the INFJ. They're good at holding grudges. INFJs may forgive but forgetting is an entirely different story.

What To Do If You're an INFJ

As an INFJ, your perfectionist side may get in the way of forming healthy friendships. While you're seeking total compatibility, you fail to realize that not everyone can see the world as you do and not everyone has the same ideas that you have. Keep in mind that since INFJ is a rare personality type, it will be difficult for you to find someone that's exactly like you. For this reason, you need to learn how to compromise. Be aware that your criteria for friendships will seem draining to most personality types.

An obstacle for building friendships is that you have a tendency to attract more attention than you would really care for. Other personality types may find your imagination and idealism irresistible. However, as an INFJ, you naturally try to avoid having this kind of influence over people. Moreover, you generally tend to avoid personality types who are attracted to this kind of influence. Keep in mind that the more these people pursue you and the more you let them, the more difficult it becomes for you to find someone you can form a strong sense of kinship with.

Chapter 3: The INFJ and Relationships and the INFJ and Parenthood

The INFJ and Relationships

"What is hell? I maintain that it is the suffering of being unable to love." - Fyodor Dostoyevsky, a famous INFJ

What do INFJs look for in a relationship?

INFJs are the type to stay away from casual relationships in favor of deeper, more meaningful romantic relationships. As a result, they will take however long it's needed to find a person with whom they can genuinely connect with. Once they do find that person, their relationship will possess a kind of depth and sincerity that most people desire.

INFJs are very picky. An INFJ will do a great many things just to seek out potential partners who share their values. Likewise, they'll do a great many things to avoid those who don't. Same as when looking for friends, INFJs want an instant, almost otherworldly connection. Because they are extra intuitive, they are almost always able to determine whether a person is meant to be with them in the long term. Additionally, they can let go of a relationship if they believe that there are better prospects out there. INFJs seek partners who are able to appreciate their imagination.

What's it like to be in love with an INFJ?

INFJs are generally desirable because of their warm and caring nature and their ability to see through a person's exterior. More than that, it's easy for them to understand others' thoughts and feelings. As significant others, they are supportive and encouraging when it comes to one's goals and achievements. INFJs are neither controlling nor yielding. Instead, they are thoughtful and appreciative of their lovers' uniqueness. They have a natural desire to maintain harmony in their marriage or relationship and thus, they are driven to resolve conflicts.

If your lover is an INFJ, remember that they have a tendency to seek perfection in relationships. As a result, potential partners must possess patience. Keep in mind that you cannot easily make an INFJ lover do something that he/she doesn't want to do especially if the act contradicts his/her core values. Lying and manipulation do not work well on people with this personality type. As previously mentioned, INFJs have the ability to see through people's motives and while they may forgive a trespass, they're unlikely to forget it. Therefore, a mistake done in the early stages of dating might very well seal your fate!

Moreover, INFJs are deep thinkers and as such, they have a tendency to withhold some of these deep thoughts. To their partners, getting them to share these contemplations can be frustrating. As mentioned, INFJS dislike conflict and will do just about anything to avoid it. For instance, they may choose to harbor feelings of jealousy rather than initiating a discussion on the issue.

When an INFJ falls in love, that kind of love is unconditional. INFJs seek to connect with their partners not just in the physical plane but in the emotional and sometimes, spiritual levels as well. Love with an INFJ has the power to defy time and distance.

What's an INFJ like in bed?

INFJs are generous, creative, and enthusiastic lovers. INFJs are not the type to go for one-night-stands. This is because brief affairs lack the emotion that they seek. They want sex to mean something. People who possess the INFJ personality type are brimming with passion and energy. Because of their spontaneity, a relationship with an INFJ is never dull. When it comes to communicating their love for their significant others, INFJs are bold and expressive. They use sexual intimacy as a means of pleasing their partners and expressing their love to them.

Which personality types are best suited for the INFJ?

Studies reveal that the personality types, which are most compatible with the INFJ, include the INFP with their "healer" feature, the ENFJ with their "teacher feature", and the ISFJ with their "protector" feature. Among the other personality types, these three are the ones most likely to share the values and interests of INFJs. Moreover, they have the highest probability of sharing the INFJs approach to life in general. While they may not always agree on everything and while they might not always get along, they have more things in common with the INFJ compared to the other personality types. That said, studies show that INFJ – INFJ matches possess the highest degree of attraction.

The INFJ and Parenthood

"Do not train a child to learn by force or harshness; but direct them to it by what amuses their minds, so

that you may be better able to discover with accuracy the peculiar bent of the genius of each." – Plato, a famous INFJ

What are INFJs like as parents?

INFJs are known to be loving and devoted parents. They have a tendency to establish strong ties with their kids. They view their relationship with their offspring as a mutual opportunity for growth and learning.

INFJ parents are tuned in to their children's emotions. They have the natural ability to see the potential in their children early on. They are keen on creating a nurturing environment, which is conducive to promoting their kids' physical, emotional as well as spiritual wellbeing. But despite the fact that they are very supportive of their children's individuality, INFJs are known to use a firm hand when it comes to disciplining them. This is especially true when concerning moral or ethical issues.

During their offspring's childhood, the INFJ parent may at first have a tendency to project his/her qualities onto the child. There's this desire for the child to have the same sense of idealism that he/she has. The INFJ parents do all that they can to ensure that their children grow up as independent and responsible adults with sound principles. For them, the ultimate parenting goal would be to raise kids who will eventually become adults with a cause. They want their children to contribute to the world. It's because of this that they want to see their children creating their own choices and forming their own beliefs.

When a child reaches the teenage phase, which is characterized by some degree of rebellion, this can be a particularly stressful period for the INFJ. Seeing their kid adopting principles that go against their own can deeply hurt the sensitive INFJs. The INFJ may feel like the child is highlighting his/her flaws as a father/mother.

Once the child reaches adulthood, the INFJ parent measure the success of parenthood on whether or not the child has developed the ability to create and live by his/her own principles. Children of INFJ parents will eventually appreciate the fact that they've been raised with proportionate amounts of freedom and accountability. In the end, INFJs are eager to someday relate with their children as equals.

Chapter 4: The INFJ and Work

"Some failure in life is inevitable. It is impossible to live without failing at something, unless you live so cautiously that you might as well not have lived at all - in which case, you fail by default." - J.K. Rowling, a famous INFJ

What is the INFJ's attitude towards work?

For INFJ, work has to have a meaning. Therefore, they thrive in careers that involve helping people. It should be a job that can provide them with the opportunity to promote their values. For this reason, people with this personality type tend to select careers in healthcare and education.

Another factor that affects an INFJ's choice of career is their thinking nature. They want a job that will allow them to apply their intellect on problems that they're interested in, most specifically problems which involve the human person. A career in psychology is a good example. That said, there are also INFJs who are have satisfactory positions in other branches of science.

Because INFJs are skilled communicators, it's also not surprising for them to obtain jobs that deal with language. INFJs are drawn to work which enable them to express themselves like blogging, writing, photography, and careers in music. No other personality type loves writing as much as an INFJ does. In fact, among the personality types, INFJs are the ones most likely to get published.

On the other hand, INFJs are not cut out for most corporate career options. However, this does not necessarily mean that individuals of this personality type have a hard time finding feasible options. On the contrary, the reason why INFJs struggle in launching a career in their 20's is because they are fully aware of the ten different career options that they can pursue. Each option is equally tempting but to the INFJ, to choose one would be to abandon all the other rich possibilities. For this reason INFs are more prone to job-hopping.

When it comes to work environments, INFJs are strongly averse to the mundane. When forced to perform routine work, the INFJ feels a lack of fulfillment. When placed in a corporate environment, INFJs will be coerced into answering to the company's and their boss's policies other than their own. As a result, they will end up aiming for leadership positions despite the fact that they dislike holding influence over people. Because of their need for independence, the may choose to begin their own practice. This way, the INFJ person will be able to work by his own rules and exercise his creativity to its maximum potential.

Compared to other personality types, INFJs care less about salary, promotion, and other recognitions like being "employee of the month". They are more motivated by the fact that they are working in accordance with their principles. They have a tendency to place less value on financial security. In other words, other people's idea of success does not apply to the INFJ. INFJs also have an inclination to be attracted to non-competitive roles.

That's not to say that INFJs lack ambition. In truth, their perfectionist personality pushes them to always strive to become better at whatever it is that they do. If you're an INFJ, then you'll understand what it's like to always believe that you are not living up to your truest potential. Despite their achievements, INFJs are at a continuous quest for self-improvement. For an INFJ, there's always room for more progress. In other words, INFJs are not the type to rest on their laurels.

In conclusion, in order to be truly happy with his career, a person with an INFJ personality has to have a job where he can practice his independence and his insightfulness and where he can help people and grow with them.

What are the best careers for INFJs?

INFJs are intrinsically clever and they may succeed in any job that they wish. But to perform a job that goes in the opposite direction of the INFJ's natural talents can be very stressful and might leave them feeling drained.

Studies reveal that most INFJs are not comfortable with jobs that require working with their hands. Such jobs include general contractor, mechanic, engineering technician, and farmer. Other positions, which individuals with this personality type might not like, include police officer, military officer, real estate broker, sales manager, financial manager, and paramedic.

Meanwhile, INFJs are most confident when taking jobs that revolve around the arts. Attractive options include editor, artist, interior designer, curator, librarian, and animator. As mentioned, the health care field is filled with appealing opportunities for the INFJ such as family physician, physical therapist, nutritionist, psychiatrist, and occupational therapist. This way, he can exercise his intellectual capabilities while satisfying his desire to contribute to the welfare of others.

It was also previously stated that INFJs do well in the educational field. It's true that even though INFJs are introverts, they gain deep satisfaction in helping other people develop. Teaching careers that are most suitable for them are those that are done on a one-on-one basis. Alternatively, they may choose to teach small groups. Examples include elementary teacher and school counselor.

Because they are good at listening to others and providing original solutions, INFJs make the best counselors. More careers for INFJs are social worker, clinical psychologist, and speech pathologist. To feed their craving for intellectual challenges while exercising their values, INFJs may consider scientific careers such as social scientist, genealogist, and environmental scientist.

If you're an INFJ who has found his way into the world of business, ideal positions would be HR manager, legal mediator, and corporate trainer.

What are INFJs like in the workplace?

As subordinates, INFJs tend to thrive in democratic and more personal managerial styles. Inflexible rules and formal hierarchy has the tendency to make the INFJ feel fidgety. As employees, they like places where their ideas are valued and where they are able to feel some degree of independence. Meanwhile, criticism can have damaging effects to the sensitive INFJ's morale. The most ideal working condition for the INFJ subordinate would be one where his boss's values are in line with his. When the perfect balance is achieved, a boss will find a dedicated, dependable, and extremely competent worker in an INFJ.

INFJ have a tendency to become popular among their colleagues. Why shouldn't they? Their optimism, eloquence, and ability to diffuse tension are all characteristics that attract people to them. However, as mentioned in the chapter about INFJs and friendships, it's not enough reason for an INFJ to be in the same workplace in order to be friends with someone. Because INFJs dislike conflict, they value cooperation over cold-blooded efficiency. And because they have a tendency to be helpful to others, some people might take advantage of this trait and shift their responsibilities to their INFJ co-worker. An INFJ might allow something like this to go on in the hope of avoiding conflict. But in the end, when the pressure becomes too much, he'll end up retreating into himself and pursuing his career goals on his own.

As mentioned previously, INFJs hate exercising authority over others. As bosses, they're certainly not the types to crack the whip. Instead, they prefer to treat their workers as equals while gaining their loyalty through motivation. However, this doesn't mean that INFJs are laidback leaders. In fact, because of this personality type's sense of equality, their expectations of their workers tend to be as high as the expectations they've set for themselves. An

INFJ loathes seeing people who are content with staying just as they are instead of aspiring for more growth and improvement.

As superiors, INFJs have the admirable feature of appreciating their employees' individual styles. They are also understanding and sensitive to their workers' needs. In the end, as long as their workers are reliable, INFJs can be great bosses who go out of their way to make their subordinates feel valued and justly compensated. But once a worker's actions undermine his values, a boss with this personality type can be unforgiving.

"It's like all those quiet people, when they do lose their tempers they lose them with a vengeance." - Agatha Christie, a famous INFJ

How to Succeed If You're an INFJ

- If you're an INFJ who's looking for your place in this world, find a job that can nurture your manifold gifts such as your ability to generate multiple possibilities when provided with a context and your ability to transform insight into an effective plan of action.

- Apart from feeding your strengths, do your best to overcome your weaknesses. For instance, you have a tendency to believe that you are always right. You also have a problem with acting in situations where quick decision-making is required.

- Make sure that you have realistic expectations of the people around you. As an INFJ, you often tend to be intolerant of other people's flaws.

- Externalize your inner thoughts. You might find it useful to discuss your ideas with other people.

- Absorb every detail in the situation before dismissing an idea too hastily.

- As an INFJ your temper can be quick and intense. When you're feeling angry, just walk away. Remember that anger can be damaging to your personal relationships and outbursts can make you look unprofessional.

- As an INFJ, it's typical of you to form an obsession over small details. Keep your eye on the goal. Your fixation on the little things is often the cause of delay.

- Learn the value of accountability. Because you are skilled in looking at a problem from various angles, you have a tendency to blame others for your problems. Remember that you are a capable problem-solver so look to yourself for solutions.

- Learn to let go and to forgive. Holding grudges can be bad for you emotionally *and* physically.

- Lighten up. Don't let your perfectionist side get the better of you. Indulge in vacations and leisurely activities. You know your idealist and altruistic personality needs to fix the world. But remember, to be able to take care of the world, you need to take care of yourself first.

Conclusion

Thank you again for downloading this book!

I hope this book was able to help you to gain an in-depth understanding of the INFJ personality and their roles as friends, lovers, parents, bosses, subordinates, and colleagues.

The next step is to use the knowledge that you have gained in this book to relate with someone who is a rare INFJ. If you're an INFJ, make use of the tips and strategies learned from this book to achieve success in your friendships, your romantic relationships, your career, and your life in general!

Finally, if you enjoyed this book, then I'd like to ask you for a favor, would you be kind enough to leave a review for this book on Amazon? It'd be greatly appreciated!

Thank you and good luck!

Here is a preview of my other book
"Self-Discipline:

Exercise your Willpower Muscle and Achieve Total Self-Control"

If you're reading this book then chances are...

- You believe that self-discipline can make a great deal of difference in your life.

- You believe that willpower is something that you can learn and develop.

- You are exploring the possibility that it's not yet too late to achieve self-discipline.

The good news is that you're on to something. However, in order to achieve self-discipline, you first need to understand where it comes from and how it works. Through the pages of this book, you'll learn about the willpower muscle, how it functions, and most importantly, *how and why it fails.*

Did you know that increasing your mental pain threshold is an effective way to help boost your self-discipline muscle? Find out how.

When mastered and applied, willpower can help you live a more productive and more meaningful life. In fact, it's the secret to much of what's good in life. It's what enables you to say no to habits that are bad for you. It's what causes you to make worthwhile sacrifices for your own good. It's the force that pushes you to become the very best version of you.

However, sheer willpower on its own is not enough. After all, self-discipline is a lifestyle. It's all about making one good lifestyle choice after another. In this book, you'll discover the steps on how to achieve long-term self-discipline. More than that, you'll find out how to develop useful strategies that will allow you to avoid and deal with temptations as they arise.

What is self-discipline and where does it come from?

Self-discipline is…

•   Your ability to delay instant gratification and resist short-term temptations in favor of your long-term goals

•   Your capacity to overrule unwelcome thoughts, emotions, or urges

•   Your ability to regulate your behavior consciously

In the simplest sense, it may be defined as your ability to do something that you know you should do regardless of whether or not you feel like doing it. We have a natural urge to go with what's easy and what's pleasurable and what's quick but self-discipline is all about being able to accomplish the more difficult, albeit necessary tasks. It's all about focusing your energy into activities that will add value into your life. The difference between successful and unsuccessful individuals is not in the tasks that they like/dislike but in their ability to move past what they like/dislike in order to achieve success.

Like everyone else, successful individuals like a couple of extra hours in bed. Who doesn't? They get up early anyway because they know that it's the price that they have to pay in order to succeed. So the question now is: How much are you willing to pay to get what you want?

Exercise your Willpower Muscle and Achieve Total Self-Control" on Amazon

Or go to: http://amzn.to/1KSoBBa

www.ingramcontent.com/pod-product-compliance
Lightning Source LLC
Chambersburg PA
CBHW062028280526
45787CB00005B/2246

* 9 7 8 1 5 1 9 2 1 2 2 2 1 *